340

A Boy Named Jesus

Jean H. Richards

Illustrated by
Paul Karch

BROADMAN PRESS
Nashville, Tennessee

Dewey Decimal Classification: J232.92
Subject headings: JESUS CHRIST—NATIVITY//JESUS CHRIST—
CHILDHOOD
Library of Congress Catalog Card Number: 77-71036
Printed in the United States of America

1

It was a special night in Bethlehem. The small city was crowded with strangers who had come to register for the new tax which the Roman rulers had made. On the rolling hills outside the city shepherds received a message from heavenly visitors.

Far away in countries to the East the Magi, or Wise Men, noticed a bright star. The star was in the constellation that their ancient teachings said concerned the Jews. The Wise Men told each other, "A great one has been born to the Jews." They prepared for a journey to see for themselves.

This special night was alive with wonder and mystery. Wonder shone in the eyes of Mary and Joseph as they looked down at the baby born only a few hours before. From the baby Jesus' face shone the light of God's love.

The events that led up to this special night began months before. Mary was a young woman who lived in Nazareth. Nazareth was a small village in Galilee. Joseph also lived in Nazareth. He was a carpenter.

Everyone in Nazareth thought well of Mary and Joseph. Joseph was the man Mary was going to marry. They both loved God and kept his laws. They were faithful in going to the synagogue and in keeping the sabbath rules. Like many faithful Jews they prayed that the Messiah would come.

Messiah means the Anointed One. The Jews believed that the Messiah would help them have again the glory King David had brought to the people of Israel hundreds of years before.

One day Mary was visited by an angel. His name was Gabriel. Mary was startled. And the words the angel spoke to her made her wonder even more. "Hail, O favored one," Gabriel said, "the Lord is with you."

Mary was frightened to be spoken to in this way. The angel continued. "Do not be afraid, Mary, for you have found favor with God." Then Gabriel said, "You will have a son. You shall call him Jesus."

This was good news to Mary. But it was also puzzling. Mary listened as the angel said more about this baby

who was to be born.

"He will be great," Gabriel told Mary. "He will be called the Son of the Most High. The Lord God will give to him the throne of his father David. And he will reign over Israel forever. There will be no end to his kingdom," the angel added.

Both Mary and Joseph could trace their ancestry back to King David. The angel was clearly talking about the Messiah. This was news that would make any Jewish woman happy—to be the mother of the Messiah.

The angel told Mary that the birth would be special, just as Jesus would be special. "The Holy Spirit will come upon you, Mary," Gabriel said, "and the power of the Most High will over-shadow you. The child to be born will be called holy, the Son of God."

The angel knew that it was difficult for people to believe messages from God. He gave Mary a sign, something which she could find out now. This would help her believe the rest of the message.

Mary had a cousin, an older woman called Elizabeth. Elizabeth was married to the priest Zacharias. They had long wanted to have a child, but they had never had children. The angel now told Mary that Elizabeth was going to have a baby. How surprised everyone would be. They all thought Elizabeth was too old to have a child.

Mary was filled with wonder. Gone was any feeling of doubt. Mary knew that God could do anything.

Although Mary was from a poor, lowly family, God was going to give this great honor to her. All people of the future would call her blessed because she was Jesus' mother. Then Mary remembered that God always blessed those who loved him and tried to follow his ways.

Mary wanted to be a servant of God. She wanted to be used to bring this wonderful event to the world. She bowed her head and told the angel, "I am the handmaiden of the Lord. May it happen to me as you have said." Yes, Mary wanted to be the mother of the baby Jesus.

The angel went away as suddenly as he had come. Mary was sure that what the angel Gabriel had said would happen. But the angel had given her a sign. Mary decided it was important for her to find out about Elizabeth for herself. She made plans for her trip to see Elizabeth.

2

Elizabeth and Zacharias lived in the hills west of Jerusalem in Judea. When Zacharias took his turn serving in the Temple, he traveled the few miles to Jerusalem.

One day Elizabeth looked up to see her young cousin Mary coming. Mary spoke a friendly word of greeting to Elizabeth.

Elizabeth was surprised. *What had brought Mary such a long way?* she wondered. Suddenly Elizabeth knew that Mary was going to have a baby. And

she knew that Mary's baby would be special. Elizabeth knew this from God. She was happy and spoke words of joy that have long been remembered. "Blessed are you among women, Mary. Blessed is the baby you will have." Then Elizabeth said to Mary, "I am honored that the mother of my Lord has come to me."

Mary looked surprised. She had been planning to tell Elizabeth about the baby, but her cousin already knew. Mary knew that God had helped Elizabeth know the news about the Messiah. Then Elizabeth said to Mary, "Blessed are you because you believed what was spoken to you from God."

Mary was humble and grateful that God had chosen her. She praised God. "I praise and rejoice in God," she said. "God who is mighty has done great things for me. Holy is his name," Mary ended her song of praise.

Mary had thought much about what the angel had said about the baby who would be born. He was to be great and have a kingdom which would never end. In the future people would be grateful to her for bringing Jesus into the world. She had a very important responsibility.

Mary stayed with Elizabeth for three months. During that time Elizabeth had many chances to talk to Mary about what had happened to Zacharias in the Temple at Jerusalem a few months before.

Elizabeth and Zacharias had long prayed to God for a child. Sometimes they wondered if God heard them or if he cared about their loneliness. But they kept their faith in God. They kept

God's laws. They performed all their religious duties. They loved God.

In the Temple at Jerusalem, the priests were divided into groups. Each group took its turn serving in the Temple worship. It was Zacharias' task to bring fire from the altar of burnt offerings, which was out in the courtyard, into the Temple and place it on the golden altar of incense. This was part of the daily worship. At this time Zacharias was alone in the Temple.

As Zacharias burned incense on the altar that stood in the holy place, the people prayed outside in the courtyard. Zacharias joined in their praying as the smoke rose.

Suddenly through the smoke Zacharias saw a form standing on the right side of the golden altar. It was an angel of the Lord. Zacharias was startled. He

became afraid. *Why was a messenger of God sent to me?* he wondered. *Was it some terrible warning?*

The angel's voice was clear. "Do not be afraid, Zacharias. Your prayer is heard. Your wife, Elizabeth, will bear you a son. You shall name him John."

Zacharias thought this was impossible. He had long ago given up the hope that one day he would have a son.

The angel was telling him great but impossible things this son would be and do. "Many will rejoice at his birth," the angel said. "He will be great before the Lord. He will be filled with the Holy Spirit even before he is born. He will turn many people to the Lord." Then the angel said, "He will prepare the people for the Messiah."

Zacharias had long wanted a son. And to have a son who would be a great religious leader was his greatest dream. The angel had said his son would prepare the way for the Anointed One. It was too wonderful for Zacharias to believe. Yet Zacharias dared not contradict God's angel.

"How shall I know this?" Zacharias asked timidly. "My wife and I are past the years when people have children."

The angel's voice lost its softness. A priest should believe God's messenger more quickly than others. "I am Gabriel," he said. "I stand in the presence of God. He sent me to you with this good news. Here is a sign to help you believe."

Then Gabriel told Zacharias that he would be unable to speak until the baby was born. And the angel left.

Outside the people were wondering what was keeping the priest inside the

Temple. It was past time for him to come out and pray the prayer that would end the service. When Zacharias came out, he opened his mouth but no sound came out. He gestured with his hands, trying to explain to the people what had happened in the Temple.

The people finally understood. They whispered excitedly to one another. "He has seen a vision. The priest had a vision from God. Now he cannot speak."

When Zacharias got home, Elizabeth was surprised and troubled that he could not talk. By gestures with his hands, Zacharias told Elizabeth he wanted a writing tablet and a pen. He wrote down what had happened.

The words of the angel were true. Elizabeth and Zacharias were going to have a baby.

3

Friends and relatives gathered around Elizabeth. She held the baby boy for them to see. Elizabeth was proud and happy.

The little boy was eight days old. It was time for the ceremony when he would receive his name and be presented to God. The friends and relatives were gathered with Elizabeth and Zacharias in the synagogue. Everyone knew that Zacharias had longed for a son. When the time came for the name to be given, the people were sure the

baby would be named after him.

"No," Elizabeth told them. "He shall be called John." Elizabeth remembered the instructions of the angel.

The people thought Elizabeth should name the child after his father or someone else in the family. "You have no relatives called John," they argued.

Zacharias still could not speak. Someone turned to him and asked, "What is the baby's name?"

Zacharias pointed to a writing tablet. Someone brought the tablet and a pen to him. Zacharias bent over the tablet and wrote, "His name is John."

All the people were surprised as they read the words. Then they were even more surprised to hear Zacharias begin to speak after months of silence.

"Blessed be the Lord God of Israel," Zacharias said. He was a proud and happy parent. He looked at the baby who was proof that God's promise had come true. All the people listened with wonder as the priest spoke. He told them that this baby was not a blessing for his family alone but for all the people of Israel.

Zacharias remembered what the angel had said about his son making ready the way for the Messiah. This meant that the ancient prophecy of the Messiah was soon to come true.

Zacharias spoke to his friends and relatives. He reminded them that God had promised that they would be delivered from their enemies. The Jews were now ruled by Rome. There was much hatred between the Jews and Romans. These soldiers from Rome were in every town. They worshiped idols rather than the true God. The Jewish people did not like some of the Roman laws, and the Romans cruelly punished anyone who disobeyed. The Jews longed to be free.

Zacharias took up the baby John and spoke to him. "You shall be called the prophet of the Most High. You shall go before the Lord and prepare his way. You will show us how we can come close to God and find forgiveness when we do wrong. You will bring us light and guide our feet into the way of peace."

At first the people who heard what Zacharias said were shocked. They did not speak. *Could it be that this ancient promise was coming true?* they wondered. Long ago they had heard that a Messiah was coming. They had also heard that there would be a special prophet to prepare his way. Were they really looking at the baby who would grow up to be that prophet?

After the ceremony, the friends and relatives went home. On the way they talked about the exciting things Zacharias had said about John. They were happy and filled with hope. When they got home, they told their friends what had happened.

"Zacharias' son was promised by an angel," they said. "The angel told them to name him John. He is going to be the prophet to make the way ready for the promised one, the Messiah. We do not have to wait long for this deliverance."

Some of the people who heard them believed at once. Others were not so sure.

4

Joseph and Mary were soon to be married. One night Joseph lay on his sleeping mat. He was thinking about the plans he and Mary had made.

When Joseph fell asleep, he had a dream. In his dream Joseph saw an angel. The angel came to him and called him by name. "Joseph," the angel said, "it is good for you to marry Mary. She will have a son. Call his name Jesus. He will save his people from their sins."

Joseph knew that the angel who spoke to him in his dream was a messenger from God. Joseph knew the angel was talking about the promised Messiah.

When Joseph woke, daylight was shining in the high window of the room. He thought about his dream and the important message. The message told him of things that would happen in the future. Joseph believed that what the angel said would come true. He was happy that he and Mary had been chosen to provide a home for the Messiah. The growing, learning years of the Anointed One would be in their hands. It was an honor, and it was a big responsibility.

Joseph and Mary continued to prepare for their wedding. People in the village were happy for them. They knew that Joseph and Mary loved each other and would make a happy home.

One day there was news from the Roman rulers. For a long time the Romans had charged the Jewish people high taxes. And now the news was that their taxes would be higher. The people in Nazareth complained. They were poor now because of taxes.

But there was more to the news from Rome. A census would be taken. Each family had to enroll for the tax in the hometown of their ancestors. This meant many families had to travel. Travel was difficult then. People either had to walk or ride mules or horses. Robbers often waited in lonely places for travelers. Few people traveled alone.

Mary and Joseph would have to travel to Bethlehem. It was a long trip, but they had to go. Mary got together the things they would need. She packed food and water for their trip. It would take about three days for them to get to Bethlehem.

Joseph got the donkey ready. Mary could ride, and he would walk. They would join other people traveling from Nazareth to Bethlehem. They would not be alone, but it would still be a hard trip.

As they made the long trip, Mary and Joseph had one happy thought. Jesus, who was soon to be born, would bring joy and gladness to the world.

5

The city was crowded. Everywhere people were pushing and shoving. And still people were coming into Bethlehem. All the inns and houses that took in travelers were full. As Mary and Joseph made their way down the narrow, winding streets, they heard people trying to find a place to spend the night.

It had been a hard trip. Mary was tired. She and Joseph knew the baby would be born soon. It was very important for them to find a place to stay.

Surely God would provide a place for them to stay.

Place after place was full. Then at one inn they found some help. This inn was full of people. Every room had as many people as it could hold. People lay on mats in the room where they ate. But the innkeeper felt sorry for Mary and Joseph. He gave them permission to stay in the stable.

During the night, a baby's cry was heard. Jesus had been born. He was well and strong. Mary wrapped the baby in the special swaddling cloths used for babies. She looked for a place to lay the baby. When she saw the manger used to feed the cattle, she knew this would make a cradle for Jesus.

Joseph put fresh straw in the manger. Mary laid the baby in the straw.

It was warm and snug for Baby Jesus. He had stopped crying. His eyes were closed. He was asleep.

Mary was glad they had found a place to stay. She looked down at the baby. Joseph looked over her shoulder. Their hearts were filled with love and joy. They remembered the words of the angel. Here was the promised one who would bring salvation to the world. As Mary and Joseph looked at Jesus, they thought of the joy and gladness they would have as they watched him grow up.

6

Judea was a warm country. Often when the nights were not too cold, the shepherds would stay out all night with their flocks of sheep. The next morning they were already near their pastures.

On this special night, there were some shepherds watching their sheep on the hills outside Bethlehem. Some of the shepherds watched to see that no sheep ran off or that no animal came up to bother the sheep. Other shepherds slept until it was their turn to watch the sheep.

Suddenly the night was bright. It was as bright as day. The shepherds were startled. Their hearts beat faster, for they were afraid. Some of the shepherds put their hands up to their eyes to keep the bright light from shining in them. The shepherds who were asleep woke up.

An angel spoke to the shepherds. "Be not afraid," he said. "I bring you good news. This news is of a great joy which will come to all the people. This day in the city of David a Savior is born." Then the angel said, "This Savior is Christ, the Lord."

The shepherds were thrilled with this news. They knew well the promise of a Savior. Now the promise had come true.

The angel went on to tell them more

about the newborn Savior. "You will find him wrapped in swaddling cloths. He will be lying in a manger."

Before the shepherds could turn to one another and say anything, the sky was suddenly filled with angels. They praised God, saying, "Glory to God in the highest, and on earth peace among men."

Then, just as suddenly as they came, they were gone. The night was once again dark. Only the moon and stars could be seen in the sky. The shepherds were excited. They were eager to go find this baby.

"Let's go to Bethlehem and see this child," one shepherd said. "Yes, let's go find this child that the Lord has told us about," another said.

A few of the shepherds stayed to care for the sheep. The other shepherds

quickly got ready and started to Bethlehem.

When they got to Bethlehem, they found the streets crowded with strangers. They asked people on every street, "Do you know of a baby that was born tonight?"

Finally, they came to the stable where Mary and Joseph and Baby Jesus were. As they looked at Mary and Joseph and then at Baby Jesus, they knew they had come to the right place. They knew this was the one the angel had told them about.

The shepherds told Mary and Joseph what had happened while they were in the fields with their sheep. They told Mary and Joseph what the angel had said.

"They said good news of a great joy?" asked Joseph.

"Yes," the shepherds told him. "And they said that it was for all the people."

Mary and Joseph looked at each other. One of the shepherds knelt beside the manger. Then the others knelt too. And they praised God for sending Jesus, the Savior.

Mary looked on quietly. She thought about all of the things that had happened. Now it was not a secret just for her and Joseph. God had spoken again. These shepherds had been told. Mary wondered what marvelous thing would happen next.

The shepherds got up. They told Mary and Joseph good-bye. Then they hurried out. They told others what had happened. The news the angel had told them was for everyone. The shepherds wanted all the people to hear.

The people listened and wondered. "Is it possible?" they asked each other. "Could the Messiah really have been born here tonight?"

Some of the people may have remembered a prophecy that told where the Messiah would be born. This prophecy said that the Messiah would come from Judea, from the city of Bethlehem. Bethlehem was the city people often called the city of David.

Other people thought the shepherds did not know what they were talking about. "I don't believe it," some of them said.

The shepherds knew what had happened. They did not worry that some people did not believe them. The shepherds went back to their sheep on the hillside. As they went, they sang praises to God.

7

When the baby was eight days old, Mary and Joseph, in a special ceremony, gave him the name Jesus. This was the name the angel had told both Mary and Joseph that the baby would be called.

Forty days later, Mary and Joseph took Jesus to Jerusalem for another special ceremony.

Mary and Joseph took Jesus to the Temple in Jerusalem. This was part of the Jewish law, and Mary and Joseph obeyed the law of their people. They also took with them a sacrifice offering for the special ceremony.

As Mary and Joseph crossed the courtyard with Baby Jesus and their sacrifice offering, they passed an old man. When the man saw them, he hurried after them.

This man was Simeon. When he caught up with Mary and Joseph, he spoke to them. He reached out his arms to hold Jesus.

Mary let him hold the baby, and Simeon began to praise God.

Simeon knew who Jesus was. This is what he said: "My eyes have seen your salvation. You have given your salvation to all people." Then he went on praising God, "Your salvation is a light to Gentiles and a glory to your people Israel."

Mary and Joseph were surprised.

Simeon explained to them. "For many years I have prayed for the Messiah to come. God told me," he said, "that I would live to see the one who was to save Israel." Simeon looked at Jesus again. "God led me here today," he said, "and when I saw this baby, I knew he was the Messiah."

Mary and Joseph were glad that they had found another person who knew that God's promise had come true. They talked with Simeon for a while. Before they left, he gave them words of blessing. But Simeon turned to Mary with a special warning. "It will not always be easy," he said. "Some will not believe in Jesus. And this will bring you unhappiness."

These last words of Simeon made both Mary and Joseph stop and think. While many people would love and praise Jesus, others would not.

While Mary and Joseph were still at the Temple, someone else spoke to them. Anna was an old woman who was known as a prophetess. She spent her time at the Temple praying and worshiping God.

When Anna saw Jesus, she too knew that he was a special baby. She knew that God had kept his promise to send the Messiah. She thanked God for sending him and for letting her see him. She told all of the people about the birth of the Messiah. "Our prayers have been answered," she said. And many people were happy at the news.

Mary and Joseph left the Temple. They had done for Baby Jesus what the Jewish law said they should do. They thought again of the people who knew that God's promise was true.

8

In the countries in the East there were special Wise Men. Sometimes they were called Magi. The kings often had wise men at their court to give them advice and to tell them if good times or bad times were coming. These men spent much time studying. They studied the stars and the planets. They studied the beliefs that told what meaning stars and dreams would have.

On the special night of Jesus' birth,

these men watched a special constellation. They thought this constellation had special meaning for the Jewish people. On this night, they saw a very bright star in this constellation. They had never seen it before. They believed that a new star told about the birth of a world leader.

"Something has happened among the Jews," they said.

"Tonight one has been born who will become king of the Jews," one of the men said. "He has been chosen by God to be a great religious leader."

The other men agreed. Some of them decided to make the journey to Judea to see for themselves. And they began to get ready for the long trip.

The Wise Men made an impressive procession with their camels and their

servants as they traveled through the country. Often they rode late into the night. And when they looked into the sky, the special star was still shining.

The Wise Men went first to Jerusalem. Jerusalem was the capital city. There Herod the king lived. He ruled Judea for the Roman government.

The Wise Men went to King Herod's palace. "Where is he who has been born king of the Jews?" they asked. "We have seen his star. We have come to worship him."

When Herod heard what the Wise Men were asking, he was troubled. A new king would be a threat to him. Herod wanted to stay king of the Jews.

As King Herod worried about the Wise Men and their question, he had a plan. First, he called wise men to his court. He also called scribes and priests from the Temple. "Come to the palace," he demanded.

When all of these men came, Herod asked them, "Where is the Messiah to be born?"

This was not a hard question for the scribes and priests to answer. They often studied the Scriptures and knew the answer. One of the men said, "He is to be born in Bethlehem."

This was all King Herod wanted to know. He sent for the Wise Men from the East. Herod was very friendly with these men. He asked them many questions about the star and where they saw it. Then Herod told them what the scribes and priests had said. "Go, look for the child," he said. "When you find him, tell me where he is. I want to go and worship him too."

All of this time, Herod had in mind his plan. He did not really want to worship Jesus. He wanted to kill him.

The Wise Men thanked King Herod and left the palace. They started toward Bethlehem. Once they were out of the busy city of Jerusalem, they looked up to the sky. There was the bright star still shining. It led them to Bethlehem, to David's city.

9

The Wise Men watched the star which had shone before them as they traveled. They watched it as they entered the city of Bethlehem.

"Look," one of the Wise Men said, "the star seems to shine directly above that small house."

The other Wise Men looked. They too saw the star above the house. They urged their camels forward. Slowly, they made their way down the narrow, cobblestone street.

As they came to the door, they looked up. They saw the star directly overhead. The Wise Men rejoiced. They were certain they had come to the right place. Eagerly they knocked on the door.

Joseph opened the door. His eyes widened in surprise at such important visitors. The Wise Men explained why they had come.

Joseph was still very much surprised. He stepped aside and asked them to come in. The Wise Men came into the house. Then they stopped. There was Mary with Jesus on her lap.

When the Wise Men saw Jesus, they knew he was a special child. They were not disappointed. They knew he was the one for whom they had been looking. How happy they were.

They knelt before him and worshiped him as they would a great king. As Mary watched them, she thought of the shepherds who had come to see the newborn baby Jesus. They too had knelt and worshiped him.

As Mary and Joseph watched, they were even more surprised. The Wise Men sent their servants out to the camels. "Bring in the special packages," they said. When the servants brought in the packages, the Wise Men took from them gifts of great value. They took gold, and the costly incense of frankincense, and the fragrant myrrh.

Again the Wise Men knelt before Jesus and held up the gifts to him. These gifts were special ones of great value.

The Wise Men did not stay long. It had been a long journey to find Jesus.

It would be a long journey home. And before they went home, they must go back to Jerusalem. They had promised to tell King Herod where to find the child.

The Wise Men were happy that night. They had found the child for themselves. They had worshiped him. They had given him the gifts they had brought. Yes, they were happy that night as they went to sleep.

But during the night they dreamed. And the dream was not a happy one. "Our dreams are warnings," they said to each other. "We must not return to King Herod. He does not want to worship Jesus. He wants to harm him."

All of the Wise Men agreed. God was telling them not to go back to King Herod. So they chose another route to go back to their own country.

Back in Jerusalem King Herod waited. Day after day passed. Still the Wise Men did not return to bring him word. Finally he realized they had tricked him. King Herod was angry. This child might grow up and try to take his place as king. Herod could not let that happen. He had first planned to kill Jesus when he found him. Now he would kill all of the baby boys in Bethlehem who were about Jesus' age. "That way," he said, "I'll be sure to get rid of the new king."

10

Soon after the Wise Men left, God sent a warning to Joseph in a dream. In this dream, an angel spoke to Joseph. He said, "Joseph, rise, take the child and his mother. Go to Egypt." The angel told Joseph to stay in Egypt until God told him to leave. "Herod is about to search for the child to kill him," the angel told Joseph.

Joseph and Mary were worried, but they were glad that God was taking

care of them. They were glad he had warned them.

Once again Mary and Joseph got ready to travel. This time they had Jesus. They traveled south, even farther away from their home in Nazareth. By the time Herod's soldiers came to Bethlehem, Mary and Joseph and Jesus were well on their way.

In Egypt, Mary and Joseph knew Jesus was safe. They were glad for that. But they missed their home and their relatives. Often they talked about their home. But they did not go back. They waited for God to tell them it was safe.

After some time, King Herod died, and his sons ruled in his place. Once again the angel came to Joseph in a dream. This time the message from God was a welcome message.

"Joseph," the angel said, "take the child and his mother and go back to your home. Those who sought the child's life are dead."

Mary and Joseph wasted no time getting ready. They were glad to be going home. They said good-bye to the friends they had made in Egypt. Then they started back to their home. They were going back to Nazareth.

As they traveled, they told Jesus, "We are going to live in Nazareth." They told him what the village was like. They told him about the countryside. They told him about the people who lived in Nazareth.

Mary told Jesus about the flowers that grew in the spring. She told him how green the grass looked after the rain. She told him about the sheep and goats he would see grazing in the fields.

Joseph told Jesus about the work he did as a carpenter in Nazareth.

Jesus listened to all that Mary and Joseph told him.

The journey had been long, but now they were home. They had friends and relatives close by. Jesus would grow tall and strong as other boys did. He would go to school at the synagogue as the other boys did. He would learn his lessons well. He would have friends among the boys and girls and the men and women. Jesus would also learn about God. It was all part of what God had planned. A boy named Jesus had been promised by God. He grew up in Nazareth and was one day known as Jesus of Nazareth.

All the hopes of Mary and Joseph and the shepherds and the Wise Men came true. Jesus showed the love of God and helped others to know God better than they ever had before.